Foreword

In a world where the dynamics of power and influence are constantly evolving, navigating the path to success requires more than just talent and determination—it demands a profound understanding of the strategies that drive achievement. As we embark on this journey through the pages of "Strategies for Success: Unlocking Your Potential" by Juan Felipe Restrepo, you are about to embark on a transformative exploration of the principles that shape our pursuit of power and influence in the modern era.

This book is not just another guide; it's a dynamic roadmap designed to help you harness your full potential and master the art of strategic influence. Whether you are an aspiring entrepreneur, a seasoned professional, or someone simply seeking to make a greater impact in your personal and professional life, this book is your key to unlocking the doors of opportunity and achievement.

Within these chapters, you will find a wealth of insights, actionable advice, and thought-provoking perspectives on the ever-shifting landscape of power and influence. Drawing from timeless wisdom and contemporary examples, the strategies presented here will empower you to:

- Develop a Clear Vision: Discover the importance of setting clear goals and defining your personal vision for success.
- Build Authentic Relationships: Learn how to cultivate meaningful connections and leverage your network effectively.
- Master the Art of Persuasion: Uncover the secrets of persuasive communication and influence.
- Navigate Challenges with Resilience: Equip yourself with the mindset and strategies to overcome obstacles on your path to success.
- Adapt to Change: Understand the role of adaptability in a world of constant change and innovation.
- Lead with Integrity: Explore the concept of ethical leadership and its profound impact on your influence.

As you delve into these pages, remember that the pursuit of success is not a solitary endeavor; it's a journey we undertake together. The wisdom contained herein is not a one-size-fits-all solution, but a versatile toolbox of ideas and strategies that you can adapt to your unique circumstances and aspirations.

I invite you to approach this book with an open mind and a willingness to embrace the transformative power of knowledge. Embrace the principles outlined within, and let them serve as your guiding stars as you set out to unlock your full potential and achieve the success you desire.

"Strategies for Success: Unlocking Your Potential" by Juan Felipe Restrepo is not just a book; it's your companion on the path to personal and professional greatness. Let the journey begin.

Best wishes,

Juan Felipe Restrepo

Table of Contents

Chapter 1

Defining Your Vision

Defining Your Vision

In the grand tapestry of success, the first thread you must weave is that of your vision. Your vision is the North Star that guides your journey through life. It's the mental image of the future you want to create, the destination toward which you'll chart your course. Without a clear vision, your efforts can become aimless, leaving you adrift in a sea of opportunities and distractions. In this chapter, we will explore the importance of defining your vision and how it serves as the foundation for all your endeavors.

The Power of Clarity

Imagine setting out on a road trip without a map or GPS. You may have a general idea of where you want to go, but without a clear route, you're likely to get lost, frustrated, and possibly never reach your destination. The same principle applies to your journey toward success. A well-defined vision acts as your road map, providing clarity and purpose to your actions.

A clear vision serves several essential purposes:

Guidance: Your vision directs your decisions and actions, ensuring they align with your ultimate goals. When faced

with choices, you can ask yourself, "Does this move me closer to or farther from my vision?"
Motivation: Having a compelling vision fuels your motivation. It gives you a reason to wake up with enthusiasm each day, knowing that you're working toward something meaningful.
Resilience: Challenges and setbacks are inevitable on the path to success. Your vision acts as a source of resilience, helping you persevere in the face of adversity.
Focus: With a clear vision, you can filter out distractions and prioritize tasks that contribute to your long-term objectives.

Crafting Your Personal Vision Statement

Defining your vision begins with introspection and thoughtful reflection. Consider these steps to craft your personal vision statement:

Reflect on Your Values: Start by thinking about your core values. What principles and beliefs are most important to you? Your vision should align with these values.
Envision Your Ideal Future: Imagine your life 5, 10, or even 20 years from now. What does it look like? What do you want to have accomplished? Visualize the details of this ideal future.
Set Specific Goals: Break down your vision into specific, actionable goals. These should be measurable and time-bound, allowing you to track your progress.

Write Your Vision Statement: Summarize your vision in a clear and concise statement. This should be a brief but powerful description of your desired future.

Remember that your vision statement is personal and unique to you. It should resonate with your deepest aspirations and provide a sense of purpose. Once you have defined your vision, it becomes a guiding light, illuminating your path to success.

In the chapters that follow, we will explore how your vision interacts with various aspects of your personal and professional life, from building authentic relationships to mastering the art of influence. Your vision is the anchor that keeps you grounded as you navigate the ever-changing seas of opportunity and challenge on your journey to success.

Defining Your Vision

Historical Examples of Influence

Throughout history, individuals with clear visions and the ability to influence others have left indelible marks on the world. These figures not only defined their own visions but also inspired countless others to follow in their footsteps. Let's explore a few notable historical examples of influential individuals:

1. Mahatma Gandhi (1869-1948)

Mahatma Gandhi's vision of nonviolent resistance and civil disobedience led to India's independence from British rule. His unwavering commitment to his vision inspired a nation to come together peacefully, despite immense challenges and oppression. Gandhi's influence extended far beyond his lifetime, shaping movements for civil rights and social justice around the world.

2. Martin Luther King Jr. (1929-1968)

Martin Luther King Jr. had a dream—a vision of a racially integrated and harmonious America. His powerful speeches and advocacy for civil rights not only galvanized the African American community but also sparked a broader movement for equality and justice. King's influence transcended his era and continues to inspire activists today.

3. Marie Curie (1867-1934)

Marie Curie's vision was to advance scientific knowledge through groundbreaking research in radioactivity. Her pioneering work not only earned her two Nobel Prizes but also laid the foundation for modern nuclear physics and medical diagnostics. Curie's dedication to her vision reshaped the field of science and paved the way for future scientific discoveries.

4. Nelson Mandela (1918-2013)

Nelson Mandela's vision was one of reconciliation and the end of apartheid in South Africa. His unwavering commitment to justice and equality, even during 27 years of imprisonment, inspired a nation and the world. Mandela's vision eventually led to the dismantling of apartheid and his election as South Africa's first black president.

5. Steve Jobs (1955-2011)

Steve Jobs had a vision of making technology accessible and user-friendly. He co-founded Apple Inc. and introduced groundbreaking products like the iPhone and iPad, revolutionizing the way we interact with technology. Jobs' innovative vision not only transformed the tech industry but also influenced design and consumer behavior worldwide.

These historical examples illustrate the power of a clear vision combined with the ability to influence others. These individuals didn't just dream; they took action, inspired others, and left lasting legacies. As you define your own vision and embark on your journey toward success, draw inspiration from these influential figures and their remarkable achievements.

Chapter 2

Building Authentic Relationships

Building Authentic Relationships

In the grand tapestry of success, relationships are the threads that connect us to the world. Our journey toward achieving our vision is rarely a solitary one. Instead, it is enriched and shaped by the relationships we cultivate along the way. In this chapter, we will delve into the art of building authentic relationships and how they become powerful pillars of support on your path to success.

The Importance of Relationships

Consider this: every person you meet, every conversation you have, and every connection you form has the potential to influence your journey. Whether you're an entrepreneur seeking partnerships, a professional navigating your career, or an individual pursuing personal growth, the relationships you nurture can make all the difference.

Here's why authentic relationships matter:

> Support and Collaboration: Authentic relationships provide a network of support. Collaborating with others can amplify your efforts and lead to innovative solutions.
> Learning and Growth: Interacting with diverse individuals exposes you to new perspectives and ideas. These encounters can be invaluable for personal and professional growth.

Opportunities: Building strong relationships often opens doors to opportunities you might not have discovered otherwise.
Emotional Well-being: Authentic connections offer emotional support, reducing stress and providing a sense of belonging.

Cultivating Meaningful Connections

Building authentic relationships isn't about collecting business cards or amassing a vast number of social media followers. It's about creating genuine, meaningful connections with others. Here are some key principles to consider:

Be Genuine: Authenticity is the cornerstone of any meaningful relationship. Be yourself, and let others see the real you. Authenticity breeds trust.
Listen Actively: Truly listening to others shows that you value their perspectives and experiences. Practice active listening by giving your full attention and asking thoughtful questions.
Empathize: Empathy is the ability to understand and share the feelings of others. It fosters deeper connections and emotional bonds.
Give Before You Receive: Building relationships isn't about immediately seeking favors or benefits. Offer your support, knowledge, or assistance without expecting anything in return.
Maintain Consistency: Consistency in your interactions helps build trust over time. Stay true to your word and be reliable in your commitments.

Show Gratitude: Express appreciation for the people in your life. A simple "thank you" can go a long way in strengthening relationships.

Navigating Professional Relationships

In the professional world, building authentic relationships can be particularly advantageous. Whether you're seeking a mentor, a business partner, or career opportunities, here are some strategies to consider:

Networking: Attend industry events, conferences, and seminars to meet like-minded professionals. Networking provides a platform for expanding your professional circle.

Mentorship: Seek out mentors who can offer guidance and share their experiences. A mentorship relationship can be invaluable for personal and career development.

Collaboration: Look for opportunities to collaborate on projects or initiatives with others in your field. Collaborative efforts can lead to innovative solutions and increased visibility.

Online Presence: Maintain a professional online presence on platforms like LinkedIn. Share your insights, engage with others, and contribute to discussions in your industry.

Remember that building authentic relationships takes time and effort. It's an ongoing process that requires genuine interest in others and a willingness to invest in the connections you form.

As you embark on your journey to success, keep in mind that the relationships you cultivate are not just a means to an end; they are a valuable part of the journey itself. They provide support, inspiration, and the potential for growth, making your path to success all the more meaningful.

Building Authentic Relationships

Historical Examples of The Art of Cultivating Authentic Connections

Throughout history, individuals who mastered the art of cultivating authentic connections have achieved remarkable success, leaving lasting legacies. Let's explore a few historical figures who exemplify this art:

1. Benjamin Franklin (1706-1790)

Benjamin Franklin was not only a Founding Father of the United States but also a master of cultivating authentic connections. He believed in the power of building personal relationships to achieve his goals. His "Junto" club, which he founded in Philadelphia, was a gathering of like-minded individuals who shared ideas and supported each other's endeavors. Franklin's ability to forge authentic connections played a crucial role in his diplomatic efforts during the American Revolution.

2. Eleanor Roosevelt (1884-1962)

Eleanor Roosevelt, the First Lady of the United States from 1933 to 1945, was known for her advocacy of civil rights, women's rights, and human rights. Her ability to connect with people on a personal level, regardless of their background, was one of her defining qualities. She traveled extensively, meeting with individuals from diverse walks of life and using her authentic connections to champion social justice causes.

3. Winston Churchill (1874-1965)

Winston Churchill, the British Prime Minister during World War II, was a masterful communicator and builder of authentic relationships. His ability to connect with both his countrymen and allies, such as U.S. President Franklin D. Roosevelt, played a crucial role in the Allied victory. Churchill's authentic connections were instrumental in forming the strong wartime alliance that ultimately defeated the Axis powers.

4. Maya Angelou (1928-2014)

Maya Angelou, the renowned poet, author, and civil rights activist, was celebrated not only for her literary contributions but also for her profound ability to connect with people on a personal level.

Her autobiographical works, such as "I Know Why the Caged Bird Sings," resonated with readers worldwide because of the authenticity and vulnerability she brought to her writing. Angelou's connections with her readers transcended cultural and societal boundaries.

5. Elon Musk (1971-Present)

In the contemporary business world, Elon Musk stands out as an example of someone who excels at cultivating authentic connections. His visionary work in companies like Tesla and SpaceX has attracted a dedicated following of supporters, employees, and partners who share his ambitious goals. Musk's ability to inspire and connect with like-minded individuals has been instrumental in driving his companies' success.

These historical figures demonstrate that the art of cultivating authentic connections is a timeless and invaluable skill. They used their ability to connect with others on a personal level to achieve remarkable goals, advocate for important causes, and inspire positive change in the world. Their examples remind us of the enduring power of genuine relationships in the pursuit of success and impact.

Navigating Professional Relationships

In the professional world, where opportunities abound and competition is often fierce, the ability to navigate and leverage professional relationships becomes a critical skill. These relationships can serve as the bridge to success, opening doors, providing guidance, and facilitating your career progression. Here, we explore the intricacies of navigating professional relationships and how to harness their potential to achieve your goals.

The Role of Professional Relationships

Professional relationships in your career can take various forms: mentors, colleagues, supervisors, clients, partners, and more. Each type of relationship offers unique benefits and opportunities:

Mentorship: A mentor can provide invaluable guidance, wisdom, and insight, helping you navigate your career path more effectively. They offer a seasoned perspective, share experiences, and can accelerate your personal and professional growth.

Colleagues: Building strong relationships with colleagues fosters a supportive work environment, enhances collaboration, and encourages knowledge sharing. Your colleagues can be valuable allies, providing assistance, feedback, and different viewpoints.

Supervisors and Managers: Nurturing a positive relationship with your superiors can lead to career advancement. Effective communication and a strong work ethic can help you stand out and earn their trust and support.

Clients and Customers: In business, client relationships are paramount. Satisfied clients become repeat customers and advocates for your products or services, ultimately driving business success.

Partnerships: Collaborative partnerships with other businesses or organizations can expand your reach, enhance your offerings, and create mutually beneficial opportunities.

Strategies for Navigating Professional Relationships

Networking: Attend industry events, conferences, and seminars to meet professionals in your field. Building a strong professional network can lead to new opportunities, collaborations, and mentorship.

Mentorship: Seek out mentors who have achieved success in your industry or profession. A mentor can provide guidance, share insights, and help you avoid common pitfalls.

Effective Communication: Develop strong communication skills, both verbal and written. Clear and concise communication fosters trust and mutual understanding.

Active Listening: Actively listen to the concerns and needs of others in your professional circle. Understanding their perspectives and challenges can help you build stronger relationships.

Conflict Resolution: Address conflicts or disagreements professionally and constructively. Effective conflict resolution can strengthen relationships rather than strain them.

Professional Development: Continuously invest in your professional development. Stay up-to-date with industry trends and cultivate expertise in your field to become a valuable resource to others.

Online Presence and Branding: In today's digital age, maintain a professional online presence. Use platforms like LinkedIn to showcase your expertise, connect with professionals, and engage in industry discussions.

Navigating professional relationships is an ongoing journey that requires diligence, empathy, and adaptability. Recognize that building these relationships is not a transactional process but a long-term investment in your career success. By nurturing authentic connections and leveraging the unique opportunities they offer, you can pave the way for personal and professional growth, opening doors to your vision of success.

In the chapters that follow, we will delve deeper into various aspects of professional relationships, from mentorship and collaboration to effective leadership and maintaining a positive online presence. Together, these skills and insights will empower you to harness the full potential of your professional connections.

Building Authentic Relationships

Historical Examples of The Transformative Power of Authentic Relationships

Throughout history, authentic relationships have played a pivotal role in shaping the course of individuals' lives and, in turn, the world around them. These relationships have the remarkable ability to transform lives and drive change. Here are a few historical examples that exemplify the transformative power of authentic connections:

1. Frederick Douglass and William Lloyd Garrison

Frederick Douglass, an escaped slave who became a prominent abolitionist and orator, formed a deep and transformative relationship with the white abolitionist William Lloyd Garrison. Garrison recognized Douglass's eloquence and authenticity, providing him with a platform to share his powerful stories and perspectives. This authentic partnership led to Douglass's rise as a leading voice in the fight against slavery, ultimately helping to shape public opinion and influence the course of history.

2. Albert Einstein and Niels Bohr

In the early 20th century, Albert Einstein and Niels Bohr, two brilliant physicists, engaged in a series of passionate and transformative debates about the nature of quantum mechanics. Despite their differing views, their authentic friendship and respect for each other's intellect fueled groundbreaking advancements in the field of theoretical physics. Their discussions laid the foundation for modern quantum theory and reshaped the way we understand the universe.

3. Susan B. Anthony and Elizabeth Cady Stanton

Susan B. Anthony and Elizabeth Cady Stanton formed an authentic and enduring partnership in the struggle for women's suffrage in the United States. Their deep friendship and shared commitment to gender equality transformed the women's rights movement. Through their collaboration, advocacy, and the formation of the National American Woman Suffrage Association, they helped pave the way for women's right to vote, one of the most significant social and political changes in American history.

4. Martin Luther King Jr. and Mahatma Gandhi

Although they lived on different continents and in different eras, Martin Luther King Jr. and Mahatma Gandhi shared a powerful bond through their commitment to nonviolent resistance and social justice. Their correspondence and admiration for each other's work amplified the impact of their respective movements for civil rights and Indian independence. Their authentic connection underscored the universal principles of peace and justice and inspired countless individuals worldwide to champion these causes.

5. Steve Jobs and Steve Wozniak

The transformative power of authentic relationships isn't limited to social and political arenas—it extends to the world of business and innovation. Steve Jobs and Steve Wozniak, the co-founders of Apple Inc., shared a deep passion for technology and a genuine friendship. Their combined talents and authentic collaboration led to the creation of groundbreaking products like the Apple I and Apple II computers, ultimately revolutionizing the technology industry and the way we interact with technology.

These historical examples demonstrate that authentic relationships can have a profound and lasting impact on individuals and society as a whole. Through mutual respect, shared vision, and a commitment to authenticity, these individuals forged connections that transcended boundaries and led to transformative change. They serve as powerful reminders of the potential for authentic relationships to shape the world and inspire positive transformation.

Chapter 3

Self-Discovery and Personal Development

Self-Discovery and Personal Development

In the quest for success, one of the most profound journeys you can embark upon is the journey of self-discovery and personal development. This chapter explores the importance of understanding oneself, identifying strengths and weaknesses, and embracing a lifelong commitment to growth and self-improvement.

The Journey Within

Imagine your life as a vast landscape, and self-discovery as the process of mapping that terrain. By understanding your inner landscape—the thoughts, emotions, strengths, and weaknesses—you gain valuable insights into the path you must navigate to achieve your goals.

The Importance of Self-Discovery

Clarity of Purpose: Self-discovery helps you define your purpose and align your goals with your authentic self. It's the compass that guides your journey.
Confidence: Understanding your strengths and weaknesses builds self-confidence. Acknowledging your abilities empowers you to tackle challenges with conviction.
Resilience: Self-discovery equips you with the tools to face setbacks and adversity. Knowing yourself enables you to adapt and bounce back with resilience.

Empathy: Understanding your own experiences enhances your ability to empathize with others. Empathy is a valuable skill in building authentic relationships and effective communication.

Identifying Strengths and Weaknesses

Strengths: Begin by identifying your strengths. These are the qualities and skills at which you excel. Leverage them to your advantage in your personal and professional pursuits.
Weaknesses: Recognize your weaknesses honestly. These are areas where you may need improvement or support. Acknowledging them is the first step toward growth.
Continuous Learning: Personal development is a lifelong journey. Seek opportunities for growth and self-improvement, whether through formal education, mentorship, or self-guided learning.

Strategies for Self-Discovery and Personal Development

Journaling: Keeping a journal allows you to reflect on your thoughts, experiences, and emotions. It can reveal patterns and insights that aid in self-discovery.
Feedback: Seek feedback from trusted friends, mentors, or colleagues. Their perspectives can provide valuable insights into your strengths and areas for improvement.
Meditation and Mindfulness: Practicing meditation and mindfulness can help you become more self-aware and in tune with your thoughts and emotions.
Goal Setting: Set clear and achievable personal development goals. These goals should align with your vision and encourage continuous growth.
Seeking Guidance: Consider working with a coach or mentor who specializes in personal development. Their guidance can accelerate your journey.

Embracing Challenges: Don't shy away from challenges or failures. Embrace them as opportunities for growth and learning. Each setback is a chance to refine your strengths and address weaknesses.

The Journey Ahead

Self-discovery and personal development are not destinations but ongoing processes. Your understanding of yourself will evolve over time, and your commitment to growth will fuel your success.

In the chapters that follow, we will delve deeper into strategies for harnessing your strengths, addressing weaknesses, and leveraging self-awareness to achieve your goals. Remember that the journey of self-discovery and personal development is a profound and empowering one—a journey that brings you closer to unlocking your full potential and achieving the success you desire.

Self-Discovery and Personal Development

Historical Examples of Self-Discovery and Personal Development

Throughout history, individuals who embarked on journeys of self-discovery and personal development not only transformed themselves but also left lasting legacies. These examples showcase the power of self-awareness and personal growth:

1. Mahatma Gandhi (1869-1948)

Mahatma Gandhi, often referred to as the "Father of the Nation" in India, is an iconic example of personal development through self-discovery. Gandhi's commitment to nonviolent resistance was rooted in his deep self-awareness and spiritual journey. He sought to understand himself, his beliefs, and his principles, leading him to embrace the philosophy of nonviolence (Ahimsa). Gandhi's transformative self-discovery not only guided his personal life but also played a pivotal role in India's struggle for independence.

2. Eleanor Roosevelt (1884-1962)

Eleanor Roosevelt's journey of self-discovery and personal development was marked by her transformation from a reserved and shy individual into a formidable advocate for human rights. Her tenure as First Lady of the United States allowed her to explore her own strengths and beliefs. Roosevelt's self-awareness and commitment to personal growth led her to become a passionate and influential champion of civil rights, women's rights, and social justice on a global scale.

3. Thomas Edison (1847-1931)

Inventor Thomas Edison is renowned for his contributions to the development of the electric light bulb, phonograph, and motion pictures. His journey of self-discovery and personal development was characterized by relentless curiosity and a commitment to learning. Edison's famous quote, "I have not failed. I've just found 10,000 ways that won't work," reflects his resilience in the face of failures and setbacks. His unwavering dedication to self-improvement and innovation reshaped the world of technology and invention.

4. Maya Angelou (1928-2014)

Maya Angelou's path to self-discovery and personal development is evident in her journey from a traumatic childhood to becoming a renowned poet, author, and civil rights activist. Angelou's autobiographical works, particularly "I Know Why the Caged Bird Sings," reflect her profound self-reflection and transformation. Through her writing and her advocacy, she inspired countless individuals to confront their own challenges and embrace personal growth.

5. Nelson Mandela (1918-2013)

Nelson Mandela's journey from prisoner to president exemplifies the power of self-discovery and personal development. During his 27-year imprisonment, Mandela engaged in deep self-reflection and embraced principles of forgiveness and reconciliation. His transformation from a political prisoner to a unifying leader played a crucial role in ending apartheid in South Africa and establishing a multiracial democracy.

These historical examples underscore the transformative potential of self-discovery and personal development. Each individual embarked on a unique journey of self-awareness, resilience, and growth, which not only enriched their lives but also left an indelible mark on the world. Their stories inspire us to explore our own inner landscapes, confront challenges, and pursue personal development as a path to success and positive impact.

Chapter 4

The Psychology of Persuasion

The Psychology of Persuasion

In the journey toward success, the ability to influence and persuade others is a potent tool. Whether you're a leader, an entrepreneur, or an individual seeking to achieve personal goals, understanding the psychology of persuasion is a valuable skill. In this chapter, we delve into the principles and strategies that underlie effective persuasion, enabling you to ethically and authentically influence others to support your vision.

The Power of Persuasion

Persuasion is the art of guiding others toward a particular belief, action, or decision. It's not about manipulation but rather the skillful presentation of information and ideas to help people make informed choices that align with your goals. Mastering the psychology of persuasion is essential for several reasons:

Building Consensus: Persuasion allows you to build consensus and garner support for your ideas and initiatives, fostering collaboration and teamwork.

Effective Leadership: Leaders who can persuade and inspire their teams are often more successful in achieving organizational goals and driving positive change.

Entrepreneurial Success: Entrepreneurs use persuasion to attract investors, gain customers, and secure partnerships, turning their visions into reality.

Personal Growth: On a personal level, understanding persuasion can help you influence your own behavior and decision-making, facilitating personal development.

The Principles of Persuasion

Several psychological principles underpin the art of persuasion.

These principles, outlined by Robert Cialdini in his influential

book "Influence: The Psychology of Persuasion," are as follows:

Reciprocity: People tend to feel obligated to return favors. By providing value or assistance first, you can create a sense of indebtedness that leads others to reciprocate.
Commitment and Consistency: Once people commit to a small action or belief, they tend to remain consistent with it. Encourage small commitments that align with your goals.
Social Proof: People are influenced by the behavior of others. Demonstrating that others have already embraced your idea or product can create a sense of trust and acceptance.
Authority: People are more likely to be persuaded by authoritative figures or experts in a given domain. Establish your expertise and credibility to enhance your persuasive influence.
Liking: People are more likely to be persuaded by those they like and trust. Building authentic relationships and rapport can enhance your persuasive abilities.
Scarcity: The idea of scarcity suggests that people desire things that are perceived as rare or in limited supply. Highlighting the uniqueness or exclusivity of your proposition can be persuasive.

Ethical Persuasion Strategies

Effective persuasion is not about coercion or manipulation but about creating win-win situations where all parties benefit. Here are some ethical strategies for persuasive communication:

Empathy: Understand the perspectives and needs of the individuals you are persuading. Tailor your message to address their concerns and desires.
Clarity: Present your ideas and proposals clearly and concisely. Avoid ambiguity and provide evidence to support your claims.
Storytelling: Stories can be powerful tools of persuasion. Craft narratives that engage emotions and illustrate the benefits of your ideas or products.
Active Listening: Listen actively to the concerns and objections of others. Address their questions and hesitations respectfully and thoughtfully.
Building Trust: Trust is the foundation of effective persuasion. Be honest, consistent, and reliable in your interactions.
Negotiation: Be open to negotiation and compromise. Finding common ground can be a persuasive strategy that benefits all parties involved.

The psychology of persuasion is a nuanced field, and mastering it takes practice and continuous learning. As you navigate your journey toward success, remember that ethical persuasion is a valuable skill that can help you build authentic relationships, inspire others to support your vision, and achieve your goals.

In the chapters that follow, we will delve deeper into specific techniques and practical applications of persuasion, empowering you to harness this skill to its fullest potential.

The Psychology of Persuasion

Historical Examples of The Psychology of Persuasion

Throughout history, individuals who mastered the art of persuasion have achieved remarkable success in various fields, from politics to business and social change. These examples showcase the application of psychological principles in persuasion:

1. Winston Churchill (1874-1965)

Winston Churchill, the British Prime Minister during World War II, was a masterful persuader known for his inspiring speeches. His famous speeches, such as "We shall fight on the beaches," employed emotional appeal and rhetoric to rally the British people during times of crisis. Churchill's ability to convey a clear vision and evoke strong emotions played a crucial role in motivating the nation to stand firm against the Axis powers.

2. Martin Luther King Jr. (1929-1968)

Dr. Martin Luther King Jr., a civil rights leader, employed the psychology of persuasion to advance the cause of racial equality and justice. His "I Have a Dream" speech delivered during the March on Washington in 1963 is a compelling example. King used rhetorical techniques, repetition, and the power of imagery to persuade the American public and policymakers to support civil rights legislation. His persuasive abilities were instrumental in shaping the civil rights movement.

3. Steve Jobs (1955-2011)

Steve Jobs, co-founder of Apple Inc., was a persuasive visionary in the world of technology and innovation. His product launches, such as the introduction of the iPhone in 2007, were masterfully orchestrated events that combined storytelling, anticipation, and product demonstration. Jobs had a remarkable ability to convince consumers that Apple's products were not just devices but life-changing experiences, effectively shaping the course of the technology industry.

4. Elizabeth Cady Stanton (1815-1902) and Susan B. Anthony (1820-1906)

Elizabeth Cady Stanton and Susan B. Anthony were pioneers in the women's suffrage movement in the United States. Their persuasive abilities were evident in their speeches and writings advocating for women's right to vote. Through their passionate and compelling arguments, they persuaded both women and men to join the suffrage movement. Their dedication to the cause eventually led to the passage of the 19th Amendment in 1920, granting women the right to vote.

5. Nelson Mandela (1918-2013)

Nelson Mandela, the anti-apartheid revolutionary and former President of South Africa, utilized persuasive communication in his efforts to end apartheid and reconcile a divided nation. During his imprisonment, he negotiated with the South African government while maintaining his principles. Upon his release, Mandela's persuasive leadership played a vital role in dismantling apartheid peacefully and transitioning to majority rule.

These historical figures demonstrate the application of psychological principles, such as emotional appeal, storytelling, and effective communication, in the art of persuasion. Their ability to inspire, mobilize, and bring about positive change serves as a testament to the enduring power of persuasion in shaping societies and achieving significant goals.

The Psychology of Persuasion

Historical Examples of The Principles of Persuasion

The principles of persuasion, as outlined by Robert Cialdini in his book "Influence: The Psychology of Persuasion," have been demonstrated effectively by historical figures in various contexts:

1. Reciprocity: Benjamin Franklin (1706-1790)

Benjamin Franklin, one of America's Founding Fathers, employed the principle of reciprocity in his diplomatic efforts during the American Revolutionary War. Franklin recognized the importance of building relationships with potential allies, including France. He initiated a reciprocal exchange of support, including military aid and diplomatic cooperation. By giving assistance and demonstrating goodwill first, Franklin cultivated strong alliances that played a vital role in securing France's support for the American cause.

2. Commitment and Consistency: Mahatma Gandhi (1869-1948)

Mahatma Gandhi's nonviolent civil disobedience campaigns, such as the Salt March, exemplify the principle of commitment and consistency. Gandhi encouraged his followers to commit to peaceful resistance as a means of achieving social and political change. Once individuals made a small commitment to this cause, like joining a peaceful protest, they were more likely to remain consistent with their commitment. This unwavering consistency contributed to the success of the Indian independence movement.

3. Social Proof: Rosa Parks (1913-2005)

Rosa Parks, a civil rights activist, demonstrated the power of social proof during the Montgomery Bus Boycott in 1955. Her refusal to give up her seat on a segregated bus sparked a citywide boycott, and others followed her lead. The collective action of thousands of African Americans and their supporters demonstrated the principle of social proof—showing that many others were also challenging segregation. This inspired further participation and led to significant changes in civil rights legislation.

4. Authority: Albert Einstein (1879-1955)

Albert Einstein, one of the most respected scientific authorities of the 20th century, used his authority to advocate for nuclear disarmament and world peace. In the aftermath of World War II, he signed the Russell-Einstein Manifesto, which called for the end of nuclear weapons testing. His endorsement as a renowned physicist lent significant authority to the anti-nuclear movement, attracting global attention and support.

5. Liking: Oprah Winfrey (1954-Present)

Oprah Winfrey, a beloved talk show host, media mogul, and philanthropist, embodies the principle of liking. Her genuine, relatable, and empathetic personality has endeared her to millions of viewers and readers. This likability has translated into significant influence, allowing her to promote causes, products, and books with remarkable success.

6. Scarcity: Apple Inc. (Founded in 1976)

Apple Inc., under the leadership of Steve Jobs, expertly applied the principle of scarcity to its product launches. By creating anticipation and portraying their products as exclusive and in limited supply, Apple generated tremendous demand for their iPhones, iPads, and other devices. Customers often lined up outside stores to be among the first to obtain these scarce, innovative products.

These historical examples showcase how influential figures and organizations have harnessed the principles of persuasion to achieve their objectives, whether in diplomacy, civil rights, social change, or business. Understanding these principles and using them ethically can enhance your ability to persuade and influence others effectively in your own pursuits.

The Psychology of Persuasion

Historical Examples of Ethical Persuasion Strategies

Ethical persuasion strategies have been employed by influential individuals throughout history to advocate for important causes, promote positive change, and create meaningful impact:

1. Mahatma Gandhi (1869-1948)

Mahatma Gandhi's commitment to nonviolent resistance, known as "Satyagraha," exemplified ethical persuasion. Gandhi's strategy involved nonviolent protest, civil disobedience, and a deep commitment to truth and justice. He encouraged followers to peacefully resist British colonial rule in India and refused to use aggressive or coercive tactics. Through ethical persuasion, Gandhi successfully led the Indian independence movement and inspired similar movements for civil rights and social justice worldwide.

2. Susan B. Anthony (1820-1906)

Susan B. Anthony, a prominent suffragette and advocate for women's rights, employed ethical persuasion strategies in her campaign for women's suffrage. Anthony's approach included organizing peaceful protests, delivering compelling speeches, and publishing persuasive writings. She emphasized the importance of women's rights while respecting the principles of democracy and nonviolence. Her ethical persuasion efforts contributed to the eventual passage of the 19th Amendment, granting women the right to vote in the United States.

3. Cesar Chavez (1927-1993)

Cesar Chavez, a labor leader and civil rights activist, employed ethical persuasion in his advocacy for farmworker rights. Chavez organized nonviolent boycotts, hunger strikes, and marches to improve working conditions for farm laborers, often among the most marginalized and vulnerable workers. His commitment to nonviolence and his willingness to endure personal sacrifices demonstrated the ethical nature of his persuasion strategies. Chavez's efforts led to significant improvements in labor conditions and rights for farm workers.

4. Malala Yousafzai (1997-Present)

Malala Yousafzai, a Pakistani activist for female education, has employed ethical persuasion to advocate for girls' education in Pakistan and around the world. Despite facing threats and violence from the Taliban, Malala continued to speak out for the right to education. Her courage, advocacy, and commitment to nonviolence earned her worldwide recognition and support. Malala's ethical persuasion strategies have inspired global initiatives to advance girls' education.

5. Nelson Mandela (1918-2013)

Nelson Mandela's commitment to reconciliation and forgiveness during South Africa's transition from apartheid to majority rule exemplifies ethical persuasion. Mandela chose to pursue truth and reconciliation instead of vengeance, leading to the establishment of the Truth and Reconciliation Commission. This approach allowed individuals to confess their past actions, seek forgiveness, and contribute to the healing process. Mandela's ethical persuasion efforts contributed to a peaceful transition to democracy and helped heal a divided nation.

6. Greta Thunberg (2003-Present)

Greta Thunberg, a young environmental activist, has employed ethical persuasion to raise awareness about climate change. Her approach involves peaceful protests, global strikes, and addressing world leaders with a clear message about the urgency of addressing climate issues. Thunberg's ethical persuasion strategies have mobilized a global youth movement demanding climate action and have put environmental issues at the forefront of political agendas.

These historical examples illustrate how ethical persuasion strategies can lead to meaningful change while upholding principles of nonviolence, justice, and respect for human rights. By employing ethical persuasion in your own endeavors, you can inspire positive action and contribute to the betterment of society and the world.

Chapter 5

Effective Communication

Effective Communication

Effective communication is the cornerstone of success in both personal and professional endeavors. In this chapter, we delve into the vital role that communication plays in achieving your goals, fostering authentic relationships, and making a positive impact in various aspects of your life.

The Power of Effective Communication

Communication is not merely about words; it encompasses listening, understanding, and conveying ideas, emotions, and information clearly and efficiently. Mastering the art of effective communication empowers you to:

> Build Authentic Relationships: Clear and empathetic communication forms the basis of strong relationships. It fosters trust, understanding, and connection with others.
> Achieve Professional Success: In the workplace, effective communication is a key driver of career advancement. It enables you to articulate your ideas, collaborate with colleagues, and influence decision-making.
> Inspire and Lead: Effective communicators have the ability to inspire and lead others. Whether you're a manager, a team leader, or an advocate for change, your communication skills can motivate and guide others.
> Resolve Conflicts: Conflict is a natural part of life, but effective communication can help resolve disputes and disagreements amicably. It promotes problem-solving and compromise.

Principles of Effective Communication

Active Listening: Listening is the foundation of effective communication. Practice active listening by giving your full attention to the speaker, asking clarifying questions, and showing empathy.

Clarity: Clear and concise communication eliminates ambiguity and reduces the chances of misunderstandings. Use simple language and structure your messages logically.

Empathy: Empathetic communication involves understanding and acknowledging the emotions and perspectives of others. Show empathy by validating their feelings and concerns.

Nonverbal Communication: Pay attention to your body language, facial expressions, and tone of voice. Nonverbal cues often convey more than words alone.

Feedback: Provide constructive feedback and seek feedback from others to improve your communication skills. Constructive criticism helps you grow and refine your approach.

Tailoring Your Message

Effective communicators understand that different situations and audiences require tailored messages. Whether you're speaking to a diverse team, delivering a presentation, or engaging in a one-on-one conversation, consider the following:

Audience Analysis: Know your audience's needs, preferences, and expectations. Adapt your communication style accordingly.

Message Clarity: Craft messages that are clear, concise, and relevant to your audience. Avoid jargon or complex language that might confuse your listeners.
Engagement: Encourage active participation and engagement from your audience. Encourage questions, discussions, and feedback.

Overcoming Communication Barriers

Communication barriers, such as language differences, cultural misunderstandings, or emotional obstacles, can hinder effective communication. To overcome these barriers:

Cultural Sensitivity: Be aware of cultural differences and practice cultural sensitivity when communicating with individuals from diverse backgrounds.
Emotional Intelligence: Develop emotional intelligence to navigate emotional barriers and respond empathetically to others' emotions.
Conflict Resolution: Learn conflict resolution techniques to address communication breakdowns and disputes constructively.

Effective communication is an ongoing journey of self-improvement. By continuously honing your communication skills and adapting your approach to different contexts, you can enhance your ability to connect with others, convey your ideas persuasively, and achieve success in your personal and professional life.

In the chapters that follow, we will explore specific communication techniques and strategies that you can apply to various situations, further empowering you to unlock your potential and achieve your goals through effective communication.

Effective Communication

Historical Examples of Effective Communication

Throughout history, individuals who excelled in the art of effective communication achieved remarkable success in various fields. These examples showcase the power of communication in building connections, inspiring change, and shaping the course of events:

1. Abraham Lincoln (1809-1865)

Abraham Lincoln, the 16th President of the United States, was a masterful communicator known for his speeches, including the Gettysburg Address and his second inaugural address. His eloquent and empathetic communication played a pivotal role in unifying a divided nation during the American Civil War. Lincoln's ability to convey complex ideas with clarity and emotion resonated with the American people and contributed to the preservation of the Union and the abolition of slavery.

2. Winston Churchill (1874-1965)

Winston Churchill, the British Prime Minister during World War II, was a powerful and effective communicator during a critical period in history. His speeches, such as "We shall fight on the beaches," inspired courage and resolve among the British people and their allies. Through his clear and passionate communication, Churchill rallied the nation to stand firm against Nazi Germany, contributing to the eventual Allied victory.

3. Nelson Mandela (1918-2013)

Nelson Mandela, the anti-apartheid revolutionary and former President of South Africa, used communication as a tool for reconciliation and nation-building. During his presidency, Mandela employed effective communication to bridge racial divides and promote unity. His willingness to listen, understand, and empathize with different groups allowed him to navigate the challenging transition from apartheid to democracy peacefully.

4. Martin Luther King Jr. (1929-1968)

Dr. Martin Luther King Jr., a civil rights leader, was renowned for his powerful and inspirational speeches advocating for racial equality and justice. His "I Have a Dream" speech during the

March on Washington in 1963 articulated a compelling vision of a racially integrated and harmonious America. Through his use of rhetoric, symbolism, and emotion, King effectively communicated the urgency of civil rights reform, sparking change and inspiring millions.

5. Mother Teresa (1910-1997)

Mother Teresa, a Catholic nun and humanitarian, communicated her mission of compassion and service through her actions and words. Her humble and selfless demeanor conveyed her dedication to helping the poor and the marginalized. Mother Teresa's communication style, grounded in empathy and simplicity, inspired countless individuals to join her in serving the needy and suffering.

6. Malala Yousafzai (1997-Present)

Malala Yousafzai, a Pakistani activist for female education, used her voice and communication skills to advocate for girls' education in Pakistan and around the world. Despite facing threats and violence from the Taliban, Malala continued to speak out for the right to education. Her clear and impassioned communication raised awareness and garnered international support, leading to global initiatives to advance girls' education.

These historical figures demonstrate that effective communication is a potent tool for change, unity, and progress. Through their ability to connect with people, convey their messages with clarity and conviction, and inspire action, they left a lasting legacy and contributed to significant social and political transformations.

Effective Communication

Historical Examples of Tailoring Your Message

Effective communicators recognize the importance of adapting their messages to suit different audiences and situations. These historical examples demonstrate the skill of tailoring messages to connect with specific groups and achieve desired outcomes:

1. Franklin D. Roosevelt (1882-1945)

President Franklin D. Roosevelt was a master of tailoring his messages to address the diverse needs and concerns of the American public during the Great Depression and World War II. Through his radio addresses known as "Fireside Chats," Roosevelt spoke directly to citizens, using simple language to explain complex economic and political issues. His empathetic communication style reassured and connected with the American people, instilling confidence during turbulent times.

2. Nelson Mandela (1918-2013)

Nelson Mandela's ability to tailor his message played a crucial role in post-apartheid South Africa's transition to democracy. During his presidency, Mandela recognized the need to address the fears and concerns of different racial groups. His message of reconciliation, forgiveness, and unity resonated with diverse audiences, facilitating the peaceful coexistence of previously divided communities.

3. Ronald Reagan (1911-2004)

President Ronald Reagan effectively tailored his message to promote conservative values and policies during his time in office. He was known for his eloquence and persuasive communication style, which appealed to a broad range of Americans. Reagan's "Morning in America" campaign message, delivered during his 1984 re-election campaign, conveyed optimism, economic growth, and national pride, striking a chord with voters.

4. Jane Addams (1860-1935)

Jane Addams, a social reformer and advocate for women's rights, tailored her message to reach audiences with varying perspectives. She founded Hull House, a settlement house in Chicago, and used her communication skills to bridge gaps between different immigrant groups and advocate for social reforms. Addams understood the importance of adapting her message to the cultural and linguistic backgrounds of the individuals she sought to help.

5. John F. Kennedy (1917-1963)

President John F. Kennedy delivered his famous "Ich bin ein Berliner" speech in West Berlin during the Cold War. By using this message, which means "I am a Berliner" in German, Kennedy conveyed solidarity and support to the people of West Berlin in the face of communist threats. His choice of language demonstrated a deep understanding of the local context and effectively communicated his commitment to Western democracy.

6. Malala Yousafzai (1997-Present)

Malala Yousafzai, an advocate for girls' education in Pakistan, tailors her message to address different audiences. Whether speaking to world leaders, students, or global audiences, Malala adapts her message to emphasize the urgency and importance of girls' education, using different tones and examples to connect with diverse groups.

These historical figures demonstrate the significance of tailoring messages to engage and resonate with specific audiences, ultimately achieving their communication goals and making a positive impact in their respective fields.

Effective Communication

Historical Examples of Overcoming Communication Barriers

Overcoming communication barriers is essential for successful interaction and collaboration. These historical examples demonstrate how individuals and organizations addressed various obstacles to ensure effective communication:

1. Helen Keller (1880-1968)

Helen Keller, who was deaf and blind from a young age, overcame significant communication barriers through her determination and the guidance of her teacher, Anne Sullivan. With Sullivan's help, Keller learned to communicate through tactile sign language and eventually mastered braille. Keller's remarkable journey of overcoming sensory limitations not only enabled her to communicate but also inspired countless others to overcome challenges.

2. United Nations (Founded in 1945)

The United Nations (UN) serves as an example of a global organization dedicated to overcoming communication barriers among nations with diverse languages and cultures. The UN employs multiple official languages, interpreters, and translators to ensure effective communication during meetings, negotiations, and diplomatic interactions. This commitment to overcoming language barriers fosters international cooperation and diplomacy.

3. Dr. Temple Grandin (1947-Present)

Dr. Temple Grandin, an advocate for autism awareness and animal welfare, overcame communication barriers associated with autism. Despite experiencing challenges with social communication, Dr. Grandin developed innovative livestock handling techniques by utilizing her unique perspective and visual thinking skills. Her work has revolutionized the livestock industry and inspired others with autism to pursue their passions.

4. King Sejong the Great (1397-1450)

King Sejong the Great of Korea recognized the importance of overcoming communication barriers among his subjects. In the 15th century, he commissioned the creation of the Korean script, Hangul, to promote literacy and communication among the Korean people. Hangul simplified writing and allowed more individuals to participate in societal and administrative affairs, enhancing communication throughout the Korean peninsula.

5. Nelson Mandela (1918-2013)

Nelson Mandela's ability to overcome communication barriers was instrumental in his efforts to unite South Africa post-apartheid. He reached out to diverse communities, including those who had been oppressors during the apartheid era, to promote reconciliation and forgiveness. Mandela's willingness to engage in open and respectful dialogue helped break down communication barriers rooted in mistrust and historical injustices.

6. Malala Yousafzai (1997-Present)

Malala Yousafzai overcame communication barriers related to gender and cultural norms in her advocacy for girls' education. Despite facing threats and violence from the Taliban, she continued to speak out for the right to education, using her voice and platform to raise awareness globally. Her resilience and unwavering commitment to her cause have helped break down barriers to girls' education in Pakistan and beyond.

These historical figures and organizations demonstrate that determination, innovation, and a commitment to understanding and adapting to unique circumstances can help overcome communication barriers. Their efforts have not only facilitated effective communication but have also inspired positive change and progress in various spheres of life.

Chapter 6

Building Your Personal Brand

Building Your Personal Brand

In the modern world, your personal brand is a powerful asset that can greatly influence your success and opportunities. Your personal brand is how you are perceived by others, and it encompasses your reputation, values, expertise, and the unique qualities that set you apart. In this chapter, we explore the importance of building and managing your personal brand to achieve your goals and make a lasting impact.

Understanding Your Personal Brand

Your personal brand is not just about how you present yourself on social media or in professional settings; it is a reflection of who you are and what you stand for. Your personal brand encompasses:

Authenticity: Your personal brand should authentically represent your values, beliefs, and personality. Authenticity builds trust and connection with your audience.
Consistency: Consistency in your actions, behavior, and communication reinforces your brand's message and identity over time.
Uniqueness: Your personal brand should highlight what makes you unique and differentiates you from others in your field or industry.

Reputation: Your reputation, built through your actions and interactions, plays a significant role in shaping your personal brand.

Building Your Personal Brand

Self-Reflection: Begin by reflecting on your values, passions, strengths, and goals. What are the key attributes you want people to associate with you? What is your unique value proposition?

Define Your Target Audience: Identify the audience you want to connect with and influence. Understanding their needs and preferences is essential in tailoring your brand message.

Craft Your Story: Narratives are powerful tools for building personal brands. Develop a compelling personal story that communicates your journey, challenges, successes, and aspirations.

Online Presence: In the digital age, your online presence is a vital component of your personal brand. Create and curate content that aligns with your brand message on social media platforms, blogs, or personal websites.

Networking: Building authentic relationships is crucial for your personal brand. Attend industry events, engage with professionals in your field, and nurture meaningful connections.

Consistency: Maintain consistency in your messaging, appearance, and behavior both online and offline. Consistency reinforces your brand identity and builds trust.

Managing Your Personal Brand

Monitor Your Reputation: Regularly assess how you are perceived by others. Seek feedback from mentors, peers, and colleagues to understand areas for improvement.

Adapt and Evolve: Personal brands can evolve over time as you gain experience and insights. Be open to adapting your brand to align with changing goals and aspirations.
Address Mistakes: Nobody is perfect. If you make mistakes or encounter setbacks, acknowledge them, learn from them, and use them as opportunities to strengthen your personal brand.
Stay True to Your Values: Uphold your core values and principles even in the face of external pressures. Your values are the foundation of your personal brand.

Building and managing your personal brand is an ongoing process that requires self-awareness, consistency, and dedication. When done effectively, your personal brand can open doors, attract opportunities, and enable you to leave a lasting and positive impression on those you encounter in your personal and professional life.

In the chapters that follow, we will explore strategies for leveraging your personal brand to achieve specific goals and navigate various aspects of your journey to success.

Building Your Personal Brand

Historical Examples of Building Your Personal Brand

Throughout history, individuals who strategically built and managed their personal brands achieved remarkable success and left lasting legacies. These historical examples demonstrate the power of personal branding:

1. Coco Chanel (1883-1971)

Coco Chanel, the iconic fashion designer, is a prime example of successful personal branding. She built a brand synonymous with elegance, simplicity, and independence. Chanel's personal brand was inseparable from her fashion empire. Her image, style, and innovative designs made her an enduring symbol of timeless chic, revolutionizing women's fashion in the process.

2. Walt Disney (1901-1966)

Walt Disney, the founder of Disney, is renowned for creating a personal brand that embodies creativity, imagination, and family entertainment. His vision and commitment to storytelling transformed Disney into a global entertainment powerhouse. Disney's personal brand not only defined the company but also influenced generations of storytellers and artists.

3. Oprah Winfrey (1954-Present)

Oprah Winfrey, a media mogul and philanthropist, has built a personal brand centered on authenticity, empathy, and empowerment. Her talk show, "The Oprah Winfrey Show," became a platform for discussing important issues and showcasing her ability to connect with diverse audiences. Oprah's personal brand extends to her media ventures, book club, and philanthropic efforts, making her a respected and influential figure worldwide.

4. Elon Musk (1971-Present)

Elon Musk, the entrepreneur and innovator behind companies like Tesla, SpaceX, and Neuralink, has crafted a personal brand associated with visionary thinking, determination, and technological advancement. Musk's ambitious goals, such as colonizing Mars and transitioning the world to sustainable energy, are integral to his personal brand. His unique ability to disrupt multiple industries has solidified his reputation as a game-changing entrepreneur.

5. Maya Angelou (1928-2014)

Maya Angelou, a renowned author, poet, and civil rights activist, built a personal brand founded on resilience, wisdom, and the power of words. Her autobiographical works, such as "I Know Why the Caged Bird Sings," revealed her personal journey from adversity to self-discovery. Angelou's personal brand as a voice for empowerment and social justice continues to inspire generations.

6. Mahatma Gandhi (1869-1948)

Mahatma Gandhi's personal brand was synonymous with nonviolent resistance, civil rights, and social justice. His unwavering commitment to nonviolence and peaceful protest during India's struggle for independence was integral to his brand. Gandhi's personal brand as a spiritual leader and advocate for human rights left a profound impact on the world and inspired similar movements for change.

These historical figures demonstrate the power of personal branding in shaping perceptions, influencing others, and leaving a lasting legacy. They strategically crafted their personal brands to align with their values, vision, and aspirations, ultimately achieving remarkable success and enduring influence.

Building Your Personal Brand

Historical Examples of Managing Your Personal Brand

Effectively managing one's personal brand requires continuous effort and adaptability. These historical examples demonstrate how individuals adeptly managed their personal brands to sustain their influence and relevance:

1. Steve Jobs (1955-2011)

Steve Jobs, co-founder of Apple Inc., was known for his ability to manage his personal brand through innovation, charisma, and a keen sense of design. Despite facing setbacks and being temporarily ousted from Apple, Jobs returned to lead the company to unprecedented success. His personal brand remained synonymous with creativity, product excellence, and visionary leadership throughout his career.

2. Nelson Mandela (1918-2013)

Nelson Mandela, the former President of South Africa, exemplified effective personal brand management during his post-apartheid leadership. Despite facing immense challenges and criticism from various quarters, Mandela consistently upheld his personal brand as a unifying and forgiving leader. He managed his brand by focusing on reconciliation and the greater good, earning worldwide respect and admiration.

3. Michelle Obama (1964-Present)

Michelle Obama, the former First Lady of the United States, has skillfully managed her personal brand through advocacy, authenticity, and grace. She used her platform to promote causes such as education, military families, and healthy living. Her personal brand is associated with strength, intelligence, and a commitment to public service, making her a respected figure even beyond her time in the White House.

4. Warren Buffett (1930-Present)

Warren Buffett, one of the world's most successful investors, has managed his personal brand through consistency, humility, and long-term thinking. Despite his immense wealth, Buffett maintains a frugal lifestyle and emphasizes the importance of integrity and ethical investing. His personal brand as a wise and approachable billionaire has contributed to his enduring influence in the financial world.

5. J.K. Rowling (1965-Present)

J.K. Rowling, the author of the "Harry Potter" series, has adeptly managed her personal brand as a writer and philanthropist.

Despite the immense success of her books, Rowling has continued to engage with fans and address important social issues. Her personal brand reflects a commitment to storytelling, imagination, and social responsibility, which has earned her enduring loyalty and respect.

6. Serena Williams (1981-Present)

Serena Williams, the tennis legend, has effectively managed her personal brand as a trailblazing athlete, entrepreneur, and advocate for gender equality in sports. Despite facing criticism and adversity, Williams maintains her personal brand as a fierce competitor and role model. Her ability to adapt, evolve, and maintain her brand's integrity has contributed to her status as a sports icon.

These historical figures demonstrate that managing a personal brand requires careful consideration, adaptability, and a commitment to core values and principles. By consistently aligning their actions with their personal brand identities, they sustained their influence and made a lasting impact on their respective fields.

Chapter 7

Embracing Resilience

Embracing Resilience

Resilience is a foundational quality that empowers individuals to bounce back from setbacks, face challenges head-on, and thrive in the face of adversity. In this chapter, we explore the significance of embracing resilience as a key strategy for navigating the ups and downs of life and achieving long-term success.

Understanding Resilience

Resilience is not just about enduring difficulties; it's about learning, growing, and thriving in the face of adversity. It encompasses several key aspects:

> Adaptability: Resilient individuals are adaptable and can adjust their strategies and approaches to meet changing circumstances.
> Mental Strength: Resilience involves mental fortitude—the ability to stay focused, positive, and determined during challenging times.
> Problem-Solving: Resilience is tied to effective problem-solving skills. It's about finding solutions and opportunities within obstacles.
> Emotional Intelligence: Understanding and managing one's emotions, as well as empathizing with others, are essential aspects of resilience.

Embracing Resilience

Develop a Growth Mindset: A growth mindset focuses on learning and improvement. Embrace challenges as opportunities to grow and develop new skills.

Cultivate Emotional Resilience: Learn to manage stress, anxiety, and disappointment. Practices such as mindfulness, meditation, and self-compassion can strengthen emotional resilience.

Build a Support System: Surround yourself with supportive friends, mentors, and colleagues who can provide guidance and encouragement during challenging times.

Set Realistic Goals: Break your long-term goals into manageable steps. Celebrate small wins along the way to maintain motivation and build confidence.

Learn from Failure: View failure as a valuable learning experience rather than a setback. Analyze what went wrong, adjust your approach, and persevere.

Maintain a Positive Outlook: Optimism can enhance resilience. Focus on the possibilities and opportunities that arise from challenges.

Benefits of Embracing Resilience

Improved Mental Health: Resilience can reduce the risk of anxiety and depression and enhance overall psychological well-being.

Enhanced Problem-Solving: Resilient individuals are better equipped to navigate complex problems and find innovative solutions.

Increased Adaptability: Resilience allows you to adjust to changing circumstances and thrive in dynamic environments.

Stronger Relationships: Resilient individuals often have healthier relationships, as they can better manage conflicts and setbacks.

Enhanced Success: Resilience is a key driver of long-term success. It enables you to persevere through challenges and setbacks on the path to your goals.

In the chapters that follow, we will explore specific strategies and techniques for developing and strengthening resilience. By embracing resilience, you can face life's challenges with confidence, adaptability, and the belief that you have the inner strength to overcome adversity and achieve your aspirations.

Embracing Resilience

Historical Examples of Embracing Resilience

Throughout history, individuals who embraced resilience demonstrated remarkable strength and determination in the face of adversity. These historical examples showcase the power of resilience in achieving extraordinary feats:

1. Helen Keller (1880-1968)

Helen Keller, who overcame deafness and blindness at a young age, is a shining example of resilience. With the guidance of her teacher, Anne Sullivan, Keller learned to communicate through tactile sign language and braille. Despite her profound disabilities, she went on to become an author, activist, and lecturer, advocating for the rights of people with disabilities and inspiring millions with her resilience.

2. Winston Churchill (1874-1965)

Winston Churchill, the British Prime Minister during World War II, exhibited unwavering resilience during the darkest days of the war. He delivered inspiring speeches and maintained a resolute spirit in the face of Nazi aggression. Churchill's resilience and resolve uplifted the British people and played a vital role in rallying the Allies to victory.

3. Malala Yousafzai (1997-Present)

Malala Yousafzai, a Pakistani advocate for girls' education, demonstrated extraordinary resilience in the face of violence and adversity. After surviving a gunshot wound from the Taliban for her advocacy, Malala continued her mission with even greater determination. Her resilience and commitment to education have made her a global symbol of courage and empowerment.

4. Nelson Mandela (1918-2013)

Nelson Mandela, imprisoned for 27 years for his anti-apartheid activism, showcased remarkable resilience. After his release, he embraced forgiveness and reconciliation, working tirelessly to dismantle apartheid peacefully and become South Africa's first black president. Mandela's resilience in the face of long-term imprisonment and injustice exemplifies the power of endurance and determination.

5. Amelia Earhart (1897-1937)

Amelia Earhart, the pioneering aviator, faced numerous challenges as she pursued her dream of becoming the first woman to fly solo across the Atlantic Ocean. Despite encountering mechanical failures and extreme weather, Earhart's resilience and courage led to her historic achievement in 1932. Her persistence in breaking gender barriers in aviation remains an enduring legacy.

6. Abraham Lincoln (1809-1865)

Abraham Lincoln, the 16th President of the United States, exhibited exceptional resilience during the American Civil War. Despite the immense challenges of leading the nation through a brutal conflict, he maintained his resolve and commitment to preserving the Union. Lincoln's resilience in the face of crisis and personal tragedy solidified his legacy as one of America's greatest leaders.

These historical figures exemplify how embracing resilience can lead to remarkable achievements and enduring legacies. Their ability to overcome adversity, persevere through challenging circumstances, and maintain unwavering determination serves as an inspiration for all those seeking to navigate life's trials and reach their full potential.

Embracing Resilience

Historical Examples of Understanding Resilience

Understanding resilience involves recognizing how individuals effectively adapt and bounce back from adversity. These historical examples demonstrate the qualities and understanding of resilience in action:

1. Charles Darwin (1809-1882)

Charles Darwin's theory of evolution by natural selection showcases an understanding of resilience in the context of the natural world. Darwin observed how species adapt and evolve over time in response to changes in their environment. His groundbreaking work emphasized the importance of resilience in the survival and success of species.

2. Anne Frank (1929-1945)

Anne Frank, a Jewish girl who went into hiding during the Holocaust, demonstrated an extraordinary understanding of resilience through her diary. Despite living in constant fear and isolation, Anne found solace in writing and used her diary to cope with the emotional challenges she faced. Her resilience and ability to find meaning in the midst of adversity continue to inspire generations.

3. Harriet Tubman (c. 1822-1913)

Harriet Tubman, a former slave and abolitionist, exemplified an understanding of resilience as she escaped slavery and subsequently led hundreds of enslaved individuals to freedom through the Underground Railroad. Tubman's unwavering determination to liberate others despite the risks and hardships showcases her deep resilience and commitment to justice.

4. Ernest Shackleton (1874-1922)

Ernest Shackleton, the polar explorer, demonstrated an exceptional understanding of resilience during his ill-fated expedition to Antarctica. After his ship, the Endurance, was trapped in ice and ultimately crushed, Shackleton and his crew endured incredible hardships for months. Through effective leadership, optimism, and adaptability, Shackleton's understanding of resilience enabled the entire crew to survive and be rescued.

5. Marie Curie (1867-1934)

Marie Curie, a pioneering scientist, faced numerous challenges in her pursuit of groundbreaking research on radioactivity. She worked tirelessly despite limited resources, discrimination against women in science, and the potential health risks of her work. Curie's understanding of resilience allowed her to make groundbreaking discoveries and become the first woman to win a Nobel Prize in two different fields.

6. Theodore Roosevelt (1858-1919)

Theodore Roosevelt, the 26th President of the United States, demonstrated a deep understanding of resilience when he embarked on an expedition down the uncharted River of Doubt in the Amazon rainforest. Despite facing extreme hardships, including illness, injuries, and the loss of members of his team, Roosevelt's determination and resilience allowed the expedition to continue and achieve its objectives.

These historical figures understood resilience in various contexts, whether in the natural world, in the face of oppression, during exploration, or in scientific discovery. Their ability to adapt, persevere, and thrive in challenging circumstances exemplifies the diverse facets of resilience.

Embracing Resilience

Historical Examples of Embracing Resilience

Embracing resilience involves actively applying strategies to bounce back from adversity and thrive in the face of challenges. These historical examples demonstrate how individuals from various walks of life embraced resilience to overcome difficulties:

1. Helen Keller (1880-1968)

Helen Keller, who overcame deafness and blindness in her early years, demonstrated remarkable resilience. With the help of her teacher, Anne Sullivan, Keller learned to communicate and acquire an education. She embraced resilience by facing her disabilities head-on, becoming a prolific author and advocate for people with disabilities.

2. Nelson Mandela (1918-2013)

Nelson Mandela's life was marked by his enduring resilience in the face of 27 years of imprisonment under the apartheid regime in

South Africa. After his release, Mandela embraced resilience by leading the nation toward reconciliation and democracy as its first black president. His capacity to forgive and work towards a peaceful transition is a testament to resilience.

3. Marie Curie (1867-1934)

Marie Curie, a pioneering scientist, faced numerous obstacles in her pursuit of groundbreaking research on radioactivity. Despite limited resources and the prevailing biases against women in science, Curie persevered. She embraced resilience by conducting groundbreaking experiments, winning two Nobel Prizes, and leaving an indelible mark on the field of science.

4. Anne Frank (1929-1945)

Anne Frank, a Jewish girl hiding from the Nazis during World War II, embraced resilience through her writing. Despite living in fear and isolation, she courageously chronicled her experiences in her diary. Her unwavering determination to maintain hope and her belief in the goodness of humanity serve as a powerful example of resilience.

5. Thomas Edison (1847-1931)

Thomas Edison, one of history's greatest inventors, encountered numerous failures in his pursuit of inventions. He famously said, "I have not failed. I've just found 10,000 ways that won't work." Edison's ability to embrace resilience by learning from setbacks and persistently pursuing his goals led to groundbreaking inventions, including the electric light bulb.

6. Elizabeth I (1533-1603)

Queen Elizabeth I of England faced formidable challenges during her reign, including political instability and threats from rival nations. She embraced resilience by displaying strong leadership, maintaining stability, and fostering cultural and economic growth. Her reign is often referred to as the Elizabethan Era, marked by flourishing arts and exploration.

These historical figures exemplify the power of embracing resilience in the face of adversity. Whether overcoming disabilities, imprisonment, discrimination, or failure, they demonstrated that resilience is a key strategy for achieving personal and societal success.

Embracing Resilience

Historical Examples of the Benefits of Embracing Resilience

Embracing resilience brings forth numerous benefits that enable individuals to not only overcome challenges but also thrive. These historical examples highlight how individuals reaped the rewards of their resilience:

1. Mahatma Gandhi (1869-1948)

Mahatma Gandhi's commitment to nonviolent resistance and civil disobedience against British colonial rule in India showcased the benefits of embracing resilience. Despite facing imprisonment, physical hardship, and opposition, Gandhi's unwavering dedication to his principles eventually led to India's independence. His resilience not only achieved his goal but also inspired movements for civil rights and social justice worldwide.

2. Franklin D. Roosevelt (1882-1945)

Franklin D. Roosevelt's leadership as the 32nd President of the United States during the Great Depression and World War II illustrated the benefits of embracing resilience in times of crisis. His ability to remain calm and determined while addressing economic hardships and wartime challenges helped instill confidence in the American people and contributed to the nation's recovery and victory.

3. Oprah Winfrey (1954-Present)

Oprah Winfrey's rise from a difficult childhood and her experiences of poverty and abuse highlight the benefits of embracing resilience. She overcame adversity through resilience, eventually becoming a media mogul and cultural icon. Oprah's resilience allowed her to connect with audiences worldwide, inspiring them to overcome their own challenges.

4. Stephen Hawking (1942-2018)

Stephen Hawking, the renowned physicist diagnosed with ALS (amyotrophic lateral sclerosis), exemplified the benefits of embracing resilience in the face of physical limitations. Despite his condition, Hawking continued his groundbreaking work in theoretical physics and cosmology. His resilience allowed him to make profound contributions to science and inspire others to pursue their passions, regardless of physical constraints.

5. Rosa Parks (1913-2005)

Rosa Parks, often referred to as the "Mother of the Civil Rights Movement," demonstrated the benefits of embracing resilience through her refusal to give up her bus seat to a white passenger in Montgomery, Alabama. Her act of defiance sparked the Montgomery Bus Boycott and became a catalyst for the civil rights movement. Parks' resilience and courage contributed to monumental social change.

6. Sir Ernest Shackleton (1874-1922)

Ernest Shackleton's leadership during the ill-fated Endurance expedition to Antarctica highlighted the benefits of embracing resilience in extreme conditions. Despite the expedition's failure and their ship being crushed by ice, Shackleton and his crew displayed remarkable resilience by enduring harsh conditions and ultimately returning to safety. Their story of survival and resilience remains an inspiration.

These historical figures reaped the benefits of embracing resilience, achieving their goals, inspiring others, and making a lasting impact on society. Their stories demonstrate that resilience is not merely about surviving challenges but also about thriving and effecting positive change.

Chapter 8

Navigating Change and Uncertainty

Navigating Change and Uncertainty

Change is an inevitable part of life, and uncertainty often accompanies it. In this chapter, we delve into the strategies and mindset needed to effectively navigate change and uncertainty, turning them into opportunities for growth and success.

Understanding Change and Uncertainty

Change is a constant in both personal and professional life. Whether it's a career transition, a shift in market trends, or a major life event, change can be daunting. Uncertainty often arises when we face the unknown or unpredictable aspects of change. To navigate change and uncertainty successfully, it's crucial to:

Embrace Adaptability: Develop the ability to adapt to new circumstances and environments. An adaptable mindset allows you to thrive in the face of change.

Maintain Resilience: Resilience is your foundation during times of uncertainty. It empowers you to bounce back from setbacks and persevere through change.

Cultivate a Growth Mindset: Adopt a mindset focused on learning and personal development. View challenges as opportunities for growth rather than threats.

Foster Flexibility: Be open to new ideas and ways of doing things. Flexibility enables you to explore new possibilities and adjust to shifting circumstances.

Navigating Change and Uncertainty

Set Clear Goals: Even in uncertain times, having clear goals provides direction and purpose. Define your objectives and adapt your strategies as needed to stay on course.

Develop Problem-Solving Skills: Effective problem-solving is essential when navigating change and uncertainty. Break complex challenges into manageable components and seek innovative solutions.

Seek Feedback and Guidance: Don't hesitate to seek feedback from mentors, colleagues, or experts. Their insights can help you make informed decisions and navigate uncertainty more effectively.

Stay Informed: Stay up-to-date with relevant information and trends. Knowledge is a valuable asset when adapting to change and making informed choices.

Manage Stress: Practice stress management techniques such as mindfulness, meditation, or physical exercise to maintain emotional well-being during uncertain times.

Maintain a Support System: Lean on your support network, whether it's family, friends, or professional connections. They can provide encouragement and perspective during challenging times.

Benefits of Navigating Change and Uncertainty

Personal Growth: Navigating change and uncertainty often leads to personal growth, as it forces you to step out of your comfort zone and learn new skills.

Adaptability: Successfully navigating change and uncertainty enhances your adaptability, making you better equipped to handle future challenges.

Resilience: Overcoming uncertainty builds resilience, helping you bounce back from setbacks more quickly.

Innovation: Change and uncertainty can spur innovation, leading to creative solutions and opportunities.

Increased Confidence: Successfully navigating change and uncertainty boosts your confidence in your ability to handle future challenges.

In the chapters that follow, we will explore specific strategies and techniques for effectively managing change and uncertainty in various aspects of your life. By embracing change as an opportunity for growth and uncertainty as a chance to demonstrate resilience, you can navigate life's transitions with confidence and purpose.

Navigating Change and Uncertainty

Historical Examples of Navigating Change and Uncertainty

Throughout history, individuals and leaders have demonstrated exceptional skills in navigating change and uncertainty, turning challenges into opportunities for growth and success. These historical examples highlight their ability to adapt, persevere, and thrive amid uncertainty:

1. Franklin D. Roosevelt (1882-1945)

Franklin D. Roosevelt, the 32nd President of the United States, navigated change and uncertainty during the Great Depression and World War II. Through his New Deal programs and inspiring leadership, he steered the nation through economic turmoil and global conflict. Roosevelt's ability to adapt policies and provide hope during challenging times demonstrated effective leadership in times of uncertainty.

2. Marie Curie (1867-1934)

Marie Curie, the pioneering scientist, faced uncertainty and challenges throughout her groundbreaking research on radioactivity. Despite limited resources and societal biases against women in science, Curie persevered. Her ability to adapt to changing research conditions and maintain her dedication to scientific discovery led to her groundbreaking work and two Nobel Prizes.

3. Nelson Mandela (1918-2013)

Nelson Mandela, the anti-apartheid leader and former President of South Africa, navigated significant change and uncertainty during the nation's transition from apartheid to democracy. His ability to forgive and embrace reconciliation rather than vengeance paved the way for peaceful change. Mandela's leadership exemplified how embracing uncertainty can lead to profound societal transformation.

4. Amelia Earhart (1897-1937)

Amelia Earhart, the pioneering aviator, faced constant change and uncertainty in her pursuit of breaking aviation records. Despite technical challenges and unpredictable weather conditions, Earhart demonstrated resilience and adaptability. Her willingness to embrace uncertainty and push the boundaries of flight made her an iconic figure in aviation history.

5. Steve Jobs (1955-2011)

Steve Jobs, co-founder of Apple Inc., navigated change and uncertainty in the technology industry. His ability to adapt Apple's product offerings, reinvent the company's direction, and launch innovative products like the iPhone showcased visionary leadership. Jobs' willingness to embrace change and take calculated risks contributed to Apple's transformation and success.

6. Harriet Tubman (c. 1822-1913)

Harriet Tubman, a former slave and abolitionist, navigated change and uncertainty as she led enslaved individuals to freedom through the Underground Railroad. Despite the danger and uncertainty of each journey, Tubman's leadership and unwavering determination guided hundreds to liberation. Her ability to adapt to changing circumstances and persevere demonstrated her resilience and commitment to justice.

These historical figures exemplify the power of navigating change and uncertainty with adaptability, resilience, and vision. Their ability to embrace challenges as opportunities for growth and progress has left a lasting legacy and inspired countless others to do the same.

Navigating Change and Uncertainty

Historical Examples of Understanding Change and Uncertainty

Understanding change and uncertainty is a crucial aspect of successfully navigating through life's challenges. These historical examples showcase individuals who possessed a deep understanding of change and uncertainty and used it to their advantage:

1. Charles Darwin (1809-1882)

Charles Darwin, the British naturalist and biologist, is renowned for his understanding of change and uncertainty in the natural world. Through his groundbreaking theory of evolution by natural selection, Darwin explained how species adapt to changing environments over time. His insights revolutionized the field of biology and contributed to a deeper understanding of the dynamic nature of life on Earth.

2. Eleanor Roosevelt (1884-1962)

Eleanor Roosevelt, the former First Lady of the United States and a prominent human rights advocate, had a profound understanding of social change and uncertainty. She used her position and influence to champion civil rights, women's rights, and international cooperation during a tumultuous period in history. Roosevelt's ability to adapt to changing social and political landscapes made her a force for positive change.

3. Albert Einstein (1879-1955)

Albert Einstein, the renowned physicist, demonstrated a deep understanding of change and uncertainty in the realm of science. His theory of relativity fundamentally changed our understanding of space, time, and the universe. Einstein's work challenged existing paradigms and showed how embracing uncertainty can lead to groundbreaking discoveries.

4. Margaret Thatcher (1925-2013)

Margaret Thatcher, the first female Prime Minister of the United Kingdom, understood the need for economic and political change during a period of uncertainty. Her policies, often referred to as "Thatcherism," aimed to transform the British economy through deregulation and privatization. Thatcher's leadership reflected a keen understanding of the need to adapt to changing global dynamics.

5. Mahatma Gandhi (1869-1948)

Mahatma Gandhi, the leader of the Indian independence movement against British colonial rule, had a deep understanding of the power of nonviolent resistance and social change. Gandhi's philosophy of satyagraha (truth force) emphasized peaceful protest and civil disobedience as a means to bring about political change. His understanding of change and uncertainty led to India's eventual independence.

6. Grace Hopper (1906-1992)

Grace Hopper, a pioneering computer scientist and U.S. Navy admiral, had a profound understanding of the rapid technological change in the computing industry. She contributed to the development of early computer programming languages and played a crucial role in the advancement of computing technology. Hopper's adaptability and understanding of technological change paved the way for innovations in computer science.

These historical figures not only understood change and uncertainty but also harnessed their knowledge to effect positive transformations in their respective fields. Their ability to adapt, embrace uncertainty, and drive change has left a lasting impact on science, society, and the world at large.

Chapter 9

Ethical Leadership

Ethical Leadership

Ethical leadership is the cornerstone of sustainable success. In this chapter, we explore the principles and practices of ethical leadership and how they contribute to personal and organizational growth.

The Importance of Ethical Leadership

Ethical leadership is not just about following rules and guidelines; it's about setting the right example and making ethical choices even when faced with difficult decisions. The benefits of ethical leadership include:

> Trust: Ethical leaders earn the trust and respect of their team members, colleagues, and stakeholders. Trust is the foundation of strong relationships and effective collaboration.
> Morale: Ethical leaders create a positive work environment where employees feel valued and respected. High morale leads to increased productivity and job satisfaction.
> Reputation: Ethical leaders and organizations with a strong ethical foundation build a positive reputation in the industry and among customers and clients.
> Long-Term Success: Ethical leadership is associated with long-term organizational success, as it fosters stability and sustainable growth.

Principles of Ethical Leadership

Integrity: Ethical leaders act with integrity by adhering to a strong moral and ethical code. They are honest, transparent, and consistent in their actions and decisions.
Respect: Ethical leaders treat all individuals with respect, valuing diversity and promoting inclusivity. They listen actively and consider different perspectives.
Fairness: Ethical leaders are fair and just in their decisions and actions. They do not favor one group or individual over others and ensure equity in opportunities and treatment.
Accountability: Ethical leaders take responsibility for their actions and decisions. They hold themselves and their team members accountable for their behavior and outcomes.
Empathy: Ethical leaders demonstrate empathy by understanding and considering the feelings and perspectives of others. They show compassion and support in times of need.

Practices of Ethical Leadership

Lead by Example: Ethical leaders set the standard by consistently acting in accordance with their ethical principles. They demonstrate the behavior they expect from others.
Communicate Ethical Values: Ethical leaders openly communicate their organization's ethical values and expectations. They create a culture of ethics through clear communication.
Encourage Ethical Decision-Making: Ethical leaders empower their team members to make ethical decisions by providing guidance and support. They foster a culture where ethical dilemmas are openly discussed.
Address Ethical Breaches: Ethical leaders promptly address ethical breaches and misconduct within the organization. They take appropriate action to rectify issues and prevent recurrences.

Seek Feedback: Ethical leaders actively seek feedback from their team members and stakeholders to gauge the ethical climate and make improvements as needed.

The Ethical Leadership Advantage

Ethical leadership is not just a moral imperative; it's a strategic advantage. Ethical leaders build strong, cohesive teams and organizations that are more likely to achieve long-term success. They create a culture where ethical behavior is valued and expected, leading to a positive impact on individuals, organizations, and society as a whole.

In the chapters that follow, we will explore practical strategies for developing and strengthening ethical leadership skills, empowering you to lead with integrity, inspire trust, and achieve lasting success.

Ethical Leadership

Historical Examples of The Foundations of Ethical Leadership

The foundations of ethical leadership are built on principles of integrity, respect, fairness, accountability, and empathy. Throughout history, leaders have exemplified these principles, leaving a lasting legacy of ethical leadership:

1. Mahatma Gandhi (1869-1948)

Mahatma Gandhi, the leader of the Indian independence movement, is renowned for his unwavering commitment to ethical principles, including nonviolence and civil disobedience. He demonstrated the foundational principle of integrity by adhering to his beliefs even in the face of adversity. Gandhi's leadership inspired a nation and ultimately led to India's independence.

2. Nelson Mandela (1918-2013)

Nelson Mandela, the anti-apartheid leader and former President of South Africa, embodied the principles of respect and fairness. He sought reconciliation and equality, advocating for the rights of all South Africans regardless of race. Mandela's commitment to these principles helped bring an end to apartheid and ushered in a new era of democracy.

3. Eleanor Roosevelt (1884-1962)

Eleanor Roosevelt, the former First Lady of the United States and a human rights advocate, practiced accountability and empathy. She held herself accountable for promoting social justice and championed the Universal Declaration of Human Rights.

Roosevelt's empathy drove her to connect with and advocate for marginalized communities around the world.

4. Abraham Lincoln (1809-1865)

Abraham Lincoln, the 16th President of the United States, demonstrated the principle of fairness during a period of great division and uncertainty—the American Civil War. His leadership aimed to heal the nation's wounds and provide equal rights to all citizens. Lincoln's commitment to fairness laid the groundwork for the Emancipation Proclamation and the eventual abolition of slavery.

5. Mother Teresa (1910-1997)

Mother Teresa, the Catholic nun and humanitarian, practiced empathy and accountability in her work with the poor and marginalized in Calcutta, India. She embraced individuals who were often shunned by society and held herself accountable for providing them with care, compassion, and dignity.

6. Martin Luther King Jr. (1929-1968)

Martin Luther King Jr., a civil rights leader, embodied integrity and respect in his pursuit of racial equality and justice. He advocated for nonviolent protest and challenged systemic racism in the United States. King's commitment to these foundational principles led to significant advancements in civil rights.

These historical figures serve as enduring examples of leaders who built their legacy on the foundations of ethical leadership. Their actions and principles continue to inspire individuals and leaders worldwide to embrace ethical leadership in their own endeavors.

Ethical Leadership

Historical Examples of Leading by Example

Leading by example is a fundamental aspect of ethical leadership. These historical examples demonstrate how individuals have effectively led by example, setting standards and inspiring others through their actions:

1. Mahatma Gandhi (1869-1948)

Mahatma Gandhi led by example through his unwavering commitment to nonviolence and civil disobedience. He personally practiced the principles he preached, living a simple life and advocating for peaceful resistance. Gandhi's dedication to his beliefs inspired millions to follow his lead in the struggle for India's independence.

2. Nelson Mandela (1918-2013)

Nelson Mandela led by example by embracing reconciliation and forgiveness as the foundation of post-apartheid South Africa. He demonstrated the power of unity by forming a government of national unity, including political opponents. Mandela's willingness to forgive his captors and work toward a racially inclusive South Africa set a powerful example for the nation.

3. Eleanor Roosevelt (1884-1962)

Eleanor Roosevelt led by example through her tireless advocacy for human rights. As the chair of the United Nations Commission on Human Rights, she played a pivotal role in drafting the Universal Declaration of Human Rights. Her personal dedication to this cause set the standard for human rights advocacy worldwide.

4. Abraham Lincoln (1809-1865)

Abraham Lincoln led by example during the American Civil War, demonstrating calmness, empathy, and resolve as the nation's leader. His leadership by example extended to his commitment to the principles of freedom and equality, culminating in the Emancipation Proclamation and the eventual abolition of slavery.

5. Mother Teresa (1910-1997)

Mother Teresa led by example through her selfless service to the poor and marginalized in Calcutta, India. She personally cared for the sick and dying, living a life of extreme simplicity and humility. Her dedication to the principles of compassion and service set a powerful example for her fellow sisters and volunteers.

6. Martin Luther King Jr. (1929-1968)

Martin Luther King Jr. led by example in his pursuit of civil rights and racial equality in the United States. He practiced nonviolent resistance even in the face of violence and oppression. King's leadership by example inspired countless individuals to join the civil rights movement and advocate for justice and equality.

These historical figures exemplify how leading by example can have a profound impact on individuals, movements, and societies. Their actions and commitment to ethical principles set the standard for those around them and continue to inspire generations to strive for positive change.

Ethical Leadership

Historical Examples of Building Trust and Credibility

Building trust and credibility is essential for effective leadership. These historical examples showcase individuals who were able to establish and maintain trust and credibility through their actions and leadership:

1. George Washington (1732-1799)

George Washington, the first President of the United States, is remembered for his unwavering commitment to honesty and integrity. He set the precedent for ethical leadership by willingly relinquishing power after two terms as president, establishing trust in the democratic principles of the United States.

2. Sir Winston Churchill (1874-1965)

Winston Churchill, the British Prime Minister during World War II, built trust and credibility through his unwavering resolve and transparency. His inspiring speeches and steadfast leadership during times of crisis earned him the trust of the British people and the admiration of the world.

3. Aung San Suu Kyi (1945-Present)

Aung San Suu Kyi, the Burmese political leader and Nobel laureate, exemplifies the importance of building trust and credibility through nonviolent resistance. Despite facing years of house arrest and political persecution, she maintained her commitment to democratic principles, earning the trust and support of the Burmese people.

4. Kofi Annan (1938-2018)

Kofi Annan, the former Secretary-General of the United Nations, was renowned for his diplomatic skills and ethical leadership. His efforts to promote peace and human rights, particularly during his role as a UN peacekeeping official, established his credibility as a global leader dedicated to the principles of justice and fairness.

5. Angela Merkel (1954-Present)

Angela Merkel, the former Chancellor of Germany, earned trust and credibility through her steady leadership and commitment to European unity. Her handling of the Eurozone crisis and the refugee crisis demonstrated her leadership qualities and ethical approach to complex challenges.

6. Nelson Mandela (1918-2013)

Nelson Mandela, the anti-apartheid leader and former President of South Africa, built trust and credibility through his willingness to forgive and embrace reconciliation. His commitment to truth and justice during the Truth and Reconciliation Commission process established a foundation of trust among South Africans as they moved toward a post-apartheid society.

These historical figures serve as powerful examples of leaders who successfully built trust and credibility through their actions, integrity, and commitment to ethical principles. Their leadership qualities not only earned them the trust and respect of their followers but also contributed to lasting positive change in their respective domains.

Chapter 10

Making an Impact

Making an Impact

Making an impact is the culmination of your journey toward success. In this chapter, we explore the strategies and mindset needed to create a positive and lasting impact on your life, your community, and the world at large.

The Power of Impact

Making an impact goes beyond personal success; it's about leaving a legacy and contributing to positive change. The benefits of making an impact include:

Fulfillment: Making a difference brings a sense of purpose and fulfillment to your life.

Influence: Impactful individuals have the ability to inspire and influence others to join their cause or share their vision.

Legacy: Impact is the foundation of a lasting legacy, ensuring that your contributions continue to benefit others long into the future.

Personal Growth: The journey toward making an impact often involves personal growth, as you acquire new skills, knowledge, and experiences.

Strategies for Making an Impact

Identify Your Passion: Start by identifying causes, issues, or areas that genuinely matter to you. Your passion is the fuel for making an impact.

Set Clear Goals: Define specific, measurable goals for the impact you want to create. Having clear objectives helps you stay focused and track progress.

Take Action: Begin with small, actionable steps toward your goals. Consistent action, no matter how modest, is the key to making a difference.

Collaborate: Impact is often amplified when you collaborate with like-minded individuals or organizations. Seek partnerships and alliances to broaden your reach.

Learn from Failure: Embrace setbacks and failures as opportunities to learn and grow. Resilience in the face of adversity is essential for making a lasting impact.

Areas of Impact

Community: Making a positive impact within your local community through volunteering, mentorship, or initiatives that address specific needs.

Profession: Impacting your industry or profession by innovating, sharing knowledge, and mentoring others.

Environment: Contributing to environmental sustainability and conservation efforts.

Education: Promoting access to education and lifelong learning, which can have a transformative effect on individuals and society.

Health and Well-being: Advocating for physical and mental health, promoting healthy lifestyles, and supporting healthcare initiatives.
Social Justice: Championing causes related to equality, diversity, and human rights to create a fairer society.

Measuring Impact

Measuring impact is essential to assess the effectiveness of your efforts. Consider using metrics such as the number of lives improved, communities positively affected, or resources allocated to your cause.

The Legacy of Impact

The impact you make transcends your lifetime. It ripples through time, influencing future generations and shaping the world in profound ways. As you reflect on your journey toward making an impact, remember that it is not only about what you achieve but also about how you inspire others to carry your legacy forward.

In the chapters that follow, we delve deeper into specific areas of impact and provide practical guidance on how to make a meaningful difference in the world. By embracing the strategies for making an impact, you can leave a lasting legacy that enhances the lives of others and contributes to a better future.

Making an Impact

Historical Examples of Leaving a Legacy

Leaving a legacy is a testament to the lasting impact one can have on the world. These historical examples showcase individuals who left enduring legacies that continue to inspire and benefit society:

1. Martin Luther King Jr. (1929-1968)

Martin Luther King Jr. left a powerful legacy through his leadership in the civil rights movement. His advocacy for racial equality and justice, as well as his famous "I Have a Dream" speech, continue to inspire generations to fight against discrimination and strive for a more just society.

2. Nelson Mandela (1918-2013)

Nelson Mandela's legacy is synonymous with reconciliation and the end of apartheid in South Africa. He left behind a legacy of unity and forgiveness, demonstrating the power of reconciliation and the importance of standing up for justice.

3. Mahatma Gandhi (1869-1948)

Mahatma Gandhi's legacy is rooted in nonviolent resistance and his role in India's struggle for independence from British colonial rule. His principles of truth and nonviolence continue to influence movements for civil rights and social justice worldwide.

4. Albert Einstein (1879-1955)

Albert Einstein's scientific legacy is profound, as his theories of relativity revolutionized our understanding of the universe. His contributions to science have paved the way for countless advancements in physics and technology.

5. Mother Teresa (1910-1997)

Mother Teresa's legacy lies in her selfless service to the poor and marginalized. She established the Missionaries of Charity, a global organization dedicated to helping those in need. Her compassion and commitment to humanitarian work continue to inspire charitable efforts worldwide.

6. Thomas Jefferson (1743-1826)

Thomas Jefferson's legacy in American history includes his role in drafting the Declaration of Independence and his advocacy for individual rights and religious freedom. His contributions to the founding principles of the United States have left an enduring legacy.

7. Marie Curie (1867-1934)

Marie Curie's legacy is marked by her pioneering work in radioactivity and her groundbreaking research on elements like radium and polonium. Her discoveries have had a profound impact on the field of science and medicine.

8. Steve Jobs (1955-2011)

Steve Jobs left a lasting legacy in the world of technology and innovation. His vision and leadership at Apple Inc. resulted in iconic products like the iPhone, iPad, and Macintosh, shaping the way we interact with technology today.

9. Leonardo da Vinci (1452-1519)

Leonardo da Vinci's legacy extends across multiple fields, from art to science and engineering. His innovations and contributions, such as the Mona Lisa and his anatomical studies, continue to influence and inspire creativity and scientific exploration.

10. Harriet Tubman (c. 1822-1913)

Harriet Tubman's legacy is intertwined with her courageous efforts as a conductor on the Underground Railroad, helping enslaved individuals escape to freedom. Her commitment to liberty and justice paved the way for future generations in the fight against slavery.

These historical figures left legacies that transcend their lifetimes, demonstrating the profound impact individuals can have on society and the world. Their contributions continue to inspire and shape the course of history, serving as reminders of the enduring power of a well-lived life.

Making an Impact

Historical Examples of Giving Back and Paying It Forward

Giving back and paying it forward are essential components of making a positive impact on society. These historical examples showcase individuals who dedicated themselves to giving back and inspiring others to do the same:

1. Andrew Carnegie (1835-1919)

Andrew Carnegie, the industrialist and philanthropist, exemplified the spirit of giving back. After amassing great wealth, he donated the majority of his fortune to establish libraries, universities, and other public institutions. His belief in the responsibility of the wealthy to contribute to the common good set a precedent for philanthropy.

2. Oprah Winfrey (1954-Present)

Oprah Winfrey, a media mogul and philanthropist, has used her platform to give back and promote social causes. She has supported numerous educational initiatives, established the Oprah Winfrey Leadership Academy for Girls in South Africa, and contributed to various charitable organizations.

3. Bill and Melinda Gates (Bill: 1955-Present, Melinda: 1964-Present)

Bill and Melinda Gates, co-founders of the Bill & Melinda Gates Foundation, have dedicated their wealth to addressing global challenges such as poverty, disease, and education. Their philanthropic efforts have made a significant impact on improving healthcare, reducing poverty, and advancing education worldwide.

4. Muhammad Yunus (1940-Present)

Muhammad Yunus, a social entrepreneur and Nobel laureate, is known for his microcredit and microfinance initiatives that have empowered millions of impoverished individuals to start small businesses. His work in social entrepreneurship has inspired similar initiatives globally.

5. Princess Diana (1961-1997)

Princess Diana of Wales used her position and fame to raise awareness about various charitable causes, including HIV/AIDS, landmines, and homelessness. Her genuine compassion for those in need inspired others to get involved in humanitarian efforts.

6. Fred Rogers (1928-2003)

Fred Rogers, known as Mr. Rogers, dedicated his career to educating and comforting children through his television program, "Mister Rogers' Neighborhood." His commitment to teaching empathy, kindness, and understanding left a lasting legacy of positive influence on children and adults alike.

7. Elie Wiesel (1928-2016)

Elie Wiesel, a Holocaust survivor and author, used his experiences to advocate for human rights and speak out against indifference and hatred. He established the Elie Wiesel Foundation for Humanity to combat injustice and promote tolerance and understanding.

8. Malala Yousafzai (1997-Present)

Malala Yousafzai, a Pakistani education activist and Nobel laureate, survived an assassination attempt by the Taliban for advocating girls' education. She has continued to advocate for girls' education worldwide, emphasizing the importance of investing in the future through education.

9. Desmond Tutu (1931-2021)

Desmond Tutu, the South African Anglican archbishop and social rights activist, played a key role in the fight against apartheid. His commitment to justice and reconciliation contributed to a peaceful transition to democracy in South Africa.

10. Jane Addams (1860-1935)

Jane Addams, a social worker and reformer, co-founded Hull House in Chicago, a settlement house that provided social services to immigrants and impoverished individuals. Her dedication to social reform and activism laid the groundwork for modern social work.

These historical figures embody the spirit of giving back and paying it forward, using their influence, resources, and dedication to make a positive impact on the world. Their actions inspire others to follow suit, creating a ripple effect of compassion and social change.

Making an Impact

Historical Examples of Measuring Your Impact

Measuring your impact is essential to understand the effectiveness of your efforts and make data-driven decisions. These historical examples showcase individuals and organizations that employed measurement and evaluation to maximize their impact:

1. Florence Nightingale (1820-1910)

Florence Nightingale, the pioneering nurse and statistician, used data and statistics to improve healthcare practices during the Crimean War. She introduced sanitary reforms based on her observations and data analysis, significantly reducing mortality rates among wounded soldiers.

2. Clara Barton (1821-1912)

Clara Barton, the founder of the American Red Cross, was known for her meticulous record-keeping and accountability. She used data to track the organization's humanitarian efforts and ensure that aid reached those in need efficiently.

3. Andrew Carnegie (1835-1919)

Andrew Carnegie, in his philanthropic endeavors, measured the impact of his donations to libraries and educational institutions by tracking the number of libraries built and the literacy rates in communities where they were established.

4. Frederick Winslow Taylor (1856-1915)

Frederick Winslow Taylor, an efficiency expert, applied scientific management principles to improve industrial processes. His time and motion studies measured worker productivity and helped increase efficiency in factories.

5. John D. Rockefeller (1839-1937)

John D. Rockefeller, the oil magnate and philanthropist, established the Rockefeller Foundation, which adopted rigorous evaluation methods to measure the impact of its philanthropic programs in various sectors, including public health and education.

6. Susan G. Komen Foundation (1982-Present)

The Susan G. Komen Foundation, dedicated to breast cancer research and awareness, employs rigorous evaluation to measure the outcomes of its initiatives. It tracks metrics related to early detection, treatment, and survivor support to gauge the impact of its programs.

7. World Health Organization (WHO) (1948-Present)

The World Health Organization collects and analyzes extensive data to assess global health trends, identify disease outbreaks, and measure the effectiveness of healthcare interventions. Their data-driven approach has been critical in improving global health.

8. Bill & Melinda Gates Foundation (2000-Present)

The Bill & Melinda Gates Foundation utilizes a results-oriented approach, tracking the impact of its investments in areas like global health, education, and poverty alleviation. They set clear metrics to measure progress and adjust strategies accordingly.

9. Muhammad Yunus and Grameen Bank (1976-Present)

Muhammad Yunus and the Grameen Bank pioneered microcredit and microfinance, providing small loans to impoverished individuals. They measure the success of their programs by tracking the financial empowerment and poverty reduction of their borrowers.

10. Save the Children (1919-Present)

Save the Children employs rigorous evaluations to measure the impact of their programs aimed at improving the lives of children worldwide. They assess outcomes related to education, healthcare, and child protection.

These historical examples demonstrate the importance of data-driven decision-making and impact measurement in various fields, from healthcare and philanthropy to education and social reform. Measuring impact allows individuals and organizations to refine their strategies, allocate resources efficiently, and maximize their positive influence on the world.

The Journey Ahead

As you reach the end of this book, you've embarked on a journey of self-discovery, personal development, and the pursuit of success through ethical leadership and meaningful impact. Your journey doesn't conclude here; instead, it marks the beginning of an exciting and transformative path ahead.

Continuing Your Personal Development

Personal development is an ongoing process that never truly ends. It's about continuously learning, growing, and evolving as an individual. Embrace the journey ahead by:

Setting New Goals: Reflect on your achievements so far and set new goals that challenge and inspire you to reach greater heights.

Embracing Change: Be open to change and adaptation. The world evolves, and your ability to adapt will be a valuable asset.

Seeking Knowledge: Continue to seek knowledge and wisdom through reading, learning from others, and expanding your horizons.

Cultivating Resilience: Strengthen your resilience in the face of adversity. Challenges are opportunities for growth.

Building Relationships: Nurture meaningful relationships and expand your network. Authentic connections are key to personal and professional success.

Sustaining Ethical Leadership

Ethical leadership is a lifelong commitment to principles that guide your actions and decisions. As you move forward, remember to:

> Lead by Example: Continue to set a positive example for others by demonstrating ethical behavior and integrity in all you do.
> Empower Others: Encourage and support those around you to make ethical choices and contribute to a culture of ethics.
> Adapt to Change: Ethical leadership is adaptable. Be ready to apply ethical principles to new challenges and opportunities.
> Measure Impact: Maintain a focus on measuring the impact of your ethical leadership to ensure your efforts make a difference.

Making a Lasting Impact

The journey ahead is an opportunity to make a lasting impact on the world. Keep these principles in mind:

> Identify Passions: Continue to explore and identify the causes and areas that matter most to you.
> Collaborate: Collaborate with others to amplify your impact and work toward shared goals.
> Measure and Adapt: Measure the impact of your efforts and adapt your strategies based on data and feedback.
> Leave a Legacy: Strive to leave a positive legacy that inspires others to make a difference and continue your work.

Remember that your journey is unique, and success is a personal pursuit defined by your values, goals, and vision. It's not about reaching a final destination but about embracing the continuous journey of self-improvement, ethical leadership, and making a meaningful impact.

As you move forward, stay true to your principles, remain open to growth and learning, and never underestimate the transformative power of your actions. The journey ahead is filled with opportunities to unlock your potential, inspire others, and create a better world. Embrace it with enthusiasm and dedication, and may your path be marked by success, fulfillment, and a positive impact on all you encounter.

Appendix: Additional Resources

In your journey toward personal development, ethical leadership, and making a positive impact, there are numerous resources available to further enhance your knowledge and skills. Here, we've compiled a list of additional resources that can aid you in your quest for success:

Books for Personal Development and Leadership:

>"The 7 Habits of Highly Effective People" by Stephen R. Covey
>"Mindset: The New Psychology of Success" by Carol S. Dweck
>"Grit: The Power of Passion and Perseverance" by Angela Duckworth
>"Leaders Eat Last: Why Some Teams Pull Together and Others Don't" by Simon Sinek
>"Daring Greatly: How the Courage to Be Vulnerable Transforms the Way We Live, Love, Parent, and Lead" by Brené Brown

Ethical Leadership Resources:

>Institute for Ethical Leadership (Rutgers University): Offers research, programs, and resources on ethical leadership.
>Center for Ethical Leadership: Provides leadership development and training focused on ethics and social justice.
>Ethical Leadership Group: Offers articles, webinars, and workshops on ethical leadership practices.

Making an Impact and Philanthropy:

Giving USA: Provides annual reports and data on charitable giving in the United States.
Effective Altruism: A movement that applies evidence and reason to determine the most effective ways to do good.
The Stanford Social Innovation Review: Publishes articles and research on social impact, philanthropy, and nonprofit management.

Learning and Skill Development:

Coursera (Coursera.org): Offers online courses from top universities and institutions on a wide range of subjects.
edX (edX.org): Provides free online courses from universities and colleges worldwide.
LinkedIn Learning (LinkedIn.com/learning): Offers a vast library of video courses on various professional and personal development topics.
TED Talks (TED.com): Features inspirational talks and presentations by thought leaders on diverse subjects.

Nonprofit and Volunteer Opportunities:

VolunteerMatch (VolunteerMatch.org): Connects volunteers with nonprofit organizations seeking assistance.
Idealist (Idealist.org): Lists job and volunteer opportunities for individuals interested in making a social impact.
All For Good (AllForGood.org): A platform for finding volunteer opportunities and events.

Social Entrepreneurship and Innovation:

Skoll Foundation (Skoll.org): Supports social entrepreneurs and innovative solutions to pressing global challenges. Ashoka (Ashoka.org): An organization that empowers social entrepreneurs to create positive change.

These resources are just a starting point on your journey toward personal growth, ethical leadership, and making a difference. Depending on your specific interests and goals, you may find additional resources and organizations that align with your mission. Remember that continuous learning and exploration are key to your success and impact.

As you engage with these resources and embark on your path, stay true to your values, embrace challenges as opportunities, and never underestimate the potential of your efforts to create positive change in the world.

Index

A

- Achievement, 24, 56, 78
- Authenticity, 42, 63, 89

B

- Building relationships, 31, 47, 67
- Business ethics, 72, 94

9 798864 020753